BE A WASTE WARRIOR

T0011463

CLOTHING WARRIOR

GOING GREEN

by Claudia Martin
Consultant: David Hawksett, BSc

BEARPORT
PUBLISHING

Minneapolis, Minnesota

Editor: Sarah Eason
Proofreader: Jennifer Sanderson
Designer: Paul Myerscough
Illustrator: Jessica Moon
Picture Researcher: Rachel Blount

Library of Congress Cataloging-in-Publication Data

Names: Martin, Claudia, author.
Title: Clothing warrior : going green / by Claudia Martin.
Description: Minneapolis, Minnesota : Bearport Publishing Company, [2021] |
   Series: Be a waste warrior! | Includes bibliographical references and
   index.
Identifiers: LCCN 2020030848 (print) | LCCN 2020030849 (ebook) | ISBN
   9781647476953 (library binding) | ISBN 9781647477028 (paperback) | ISBN
   9781647477097 (ebook)
Subjects: LCSH: Clothing trade—Environmental aspects—Juvenile literature.
   | Refuse and refuse disposal—Juvenile literature.
Classification: LCC TT497 .M27 2021 (print) | LCC TT497 (ebook) | DDC
   338.4/7687—dc23
LC record available at https://lccn.loc.gov/2020030848
LC ebook record available at https://lccn.loc.gov/2020030849

For more information, write to Bearport Publishing, 5357 Penn Avenue South, Minneapolis, MN 55419. Printed in the United States of America.

CONTENTS

THE BATTLE TO SAVE EARTH!

Have you ever decided to change your fashion style? Or looked in your closet to find you've outgrown last year's clothes? Tossed-out clothes and shoes are a big part of the problem of global waste. Be a waste warrior to help stop this **pollution**. Even making some small changes can make a big difference.

The Three Problems with Waste

Heaps of Garbage Much of our garbage is thrown into **landfills**. But when waste breaks down in landfills, it can harm our environment. **Plastic** found in some clothing and shoes can leak harmful things into the soil and air. Waste in landfills lets off a gas called methane as it breaks down. On top of that, the waste in landfills just sits there, stored up for a future generation to deal with. That is why waste warriors avoid creating waste!

We have created landfills to deal with our huge amounts of waste.

Wasted Resources When we throw clothes away, we often get new clothes to replace them. But a lot goes into making new clothes. For example, each new **cotton** T-shirt comes from cotton plants that must be grown and watered, using our planet's limited **natural resources**.

Polluted Planet We create pollution when we burn **fossil fuels**, such as **coal** and **oil**, to power factories that make all kinds of products, from fabrics to sneakers. When fossil fuels are burned, they release **carbon dioxide** and other gases that trap the sun's heat around our planet. This causes temperatures to rise and climates to change.

Pollution from factories is a key cause of **global warming** and **climate change**.

On average, it takes 713 gallons (2,700 L) of water to produce the cotton for just one T-shirt.

The Six Rs

So how can you help? Here are six ways eco warriors can battle against waste. But you don't need to master them all to make a difference. Every little bit helps!

Refuse If you have a choice, say no thanks to extra packaging and bags when you're shopping.

Reduce Try to get more clothes only when you have grown out of the old ones.

Reuse Before throwing outgrown clothes in the trash, consider whether someone else could wear them.

When your pants are too short and your sweaters are too tight, consider donating them.

Repair Try fixing old, torn clothes rather than throwing them out. You may need to ask an adult for help.

Recycle Aim to **recycle** all shoe boxes and unwearable clothes, so they can be made into something new.

Rot Put ripped and unusable cotton and other **natural fabrics** in the **compost** so they will rot away.

Fixing old clothes is a simple way to reduce clothing waste.

Bring your own fabric shopping bag so you can refuse plastic bags.

NO
PLASTIC

PASS IT ON

When you get a tear in your top, do you toss it? What about if you outgrow your outerwear? A lot of clothing ends up in landfills. But almost all unwanted clothing could be reused, recycled, or **upcycled**. So let's avoid fashion disaster!

Given enough time, natural fabrics made from plant or animal hair can rot in a process called **biodegrading**. This natural process is not harmful. But when natural fabrics are put in a landfill, they are squashed tightly next to a lot of other waste, with very little air in between. In this almost-airless environment, the waste gives off methane gas as it breaks down. Methane gas traps heat around Earth. This raises global temperatures, causing climate change. While some modern landfills trap the gas, other landfills do not.

Rising temperatures are changing weather patterns across the world. Some places are facing more storms and floods, while others are experiencing serious droughts.

Ripped and stained clothes can be turned into filling for mattresses or sleeping bags.

What a Waste!

Every year, around 21 billion pounds (9.5 billion kg) of fabric winds up in U.S. landfills.

When you grow out of clothes, ask an adult to help you decide what to do with them. Can some be given to friends or family members who could wear them? Which items can be donated to thrift stores, and which are too stained or torn to be worn again? For clothes you can't give away, think about ways to reuse the fabric so it doesn't end up in the trash. You might be able to make a cool craft! Some places even let you recycle old clothes. Ask an adult to help you go online to find nearby clothing recycling programs.

Warriors Can Try:

Upcycle unwearable clothes into useful items.

- Cut them into cleaning rags.
- Braid them into bracelets or rugs.
- Make them into a bed or a toy for your pet.
- Stitch them into patches for other clothes with holes.

Donating clothes reduces waste and makes you feel good. Way to go, Waste Warrior!

A pair of jeans and a belt can be upcycled into a cool purse.

DONATIONS

WEAR OUT YOUR JEANS

Do you have a favorite pair of jeans? Many people do! But making jeans uses a lot of precious resources, from water to **fuel**.

Jeans are made of cotton, which comes from the fluffy seed heads of cotton plants. Cotton is frequently grown in hot, dry regions where it must be watered a lot. The cotton is often dyed blue to give blue jeans their signature color. But afterward, some of the remaining dye may be released into local waterways, where it harms plants and fish. Finally, the finished jeans are transported by boat or plane, often across the world, using up fuel and polluting the air. Turns out that making your favorite pants can be quite a waste! What's a waste warrior to do?

Cotton is the world's most widely grown nonfood crop.

Cotton threads
are made from
cottonseed heads,
which are called bolls.

What a
Waste!

It takes 1,800 gal (8,180 L)
of water to grow the cotton
for just one pair of jeans.

To reduce the waste from making new jeans, try washing your jeans only when really necessary. Washing them less often will give them a longer life. But what if they start to smell or are a little bit dirty? Hang them up to air and spot clean any little dirty spots! What if they rip? Ask an adult to help you patch them. If your jeans get too short, cut them into capris or shorts. Use fashion to save the planet!

Warriors Can Try:

When you've gotten every bit of wear out of your old jeans, consider low-waste options when picking out new ones.

- Secondhand jeans passed down from someone else mean new cotton doesn't need to be grown.

- Jeans made with recycled fabric reduces the need to grow cotton.

- Dark wash jeans don't use as much water for fading and distressing.

Luckily, most jeans look better the longer they are worn!

When your jeans are too short and ripped to be worn, upcycle them into something useful and fun, such as this bag.

STOP MICROFIBERS

Microfibers are tiny threads, too small to see with the human eye, that come off fabrics when they are washed. And some microfibers contain plastic. This plastic waste is rinsed down the drain and into Earth's waterways. *Yuck!*

During washing, plastic microfibers are released from plastic-based fabrics such as polyester, acrylic, and nylon. Microfibers are too small to be caught when we treat used water, so they end up in lakes, rivers, and oceans. When fish eat microfibers, the plastic can gather in their stomachs, making them feel too full to eat enough real food. But you can help reduce the amount of microfibers in the environment by making wise choices.

Fish eat plastic microfibers. Then whatever eats the fish eats plastic, too!

What a Waste!

An average load of laundry releases about nine million microfibers.

Few people realize that every time they do laundry, tiny, harmful microfibers wash away and pollute our planet.

What can a waste warrior do about plastic microfibers? Many of us already own clothes made from polyester, acrylic, and nylon. So how can we stop releasing so many microfibers into the environment? One solution is to handwash clothes made from plastic **fibers** instead of putting them in a washing machine. Your hands are gentler than the machine, so you will rub off fewer fibers. When it's time to get new clothes, try to avoid any that contain plastic fibers.

Warriors Can Try:

Whenever possible, choose clothes made from natural fabrics.

- Animal hair or products, such as cashmere, silk, and wool

- Grasses, such as bamboo

- Plant seed heads, such as cotton

- Plant stems, such as hemp and linen

- Wood, such as lyocell, modal, and rayon

Hemp fiber is a natural material that can be used to make clothing.

Sheep wool can
be knitted into sweaters
and scarves. The United States
is the world's third-biggest
producer of wool, behind
Australia and China.

GET SNEAKER SMART

Most sneakers contain a lot of parts made from plastic, including soles, stripes, and the springy foam inside. Discarded sneakers create a lot of waste.

Plastic is difficult and expensive to recycle. Materials such as glass and metal can easily be melted and reshaped into new products. But most plastics need to be ground up, then melted, then mixed with extra materials to make them useable. That's why so many unwanted sneakers end up in landfills.

Sneaker soles are often filled with a springy plastic foam.

Making matters worse, plastic does not biodegrade quickly like natural materials. In fact, sneakers can take up to 1,000 years to break down! And as they break down, they will give off harmful materials.

Fewer than 5 percent of all shoes are recycled.

What a Waste!

People in the United States throw away 300 million pairs of shoes every year.

The easiest way to reduce sneaker waste is to buy fewer pairs. Try to get new sneakers only when you've outgrown or broken the old ones. And be sure to donate old shoes that can still be worn. While you're at it, try finding your replacement pair of shoes at the thrift store! If you are shopping for new shoes, keep a lookout for eco-friendly sneakers made from recycled plastic waste or from natural materials. Some stores offer recycling bins for shoes that are too broken down to be worn again. The plastic in these old shoes can be turned into soft surfaces for playgrounds and running tracks. Talk about paving the way!

Warriors Can Try:

If your favorite sneaker company doesn't make an eco-friendly option, try writing to them to ask for a change.

- Explain why you think sneaker waste is a problem.
- Offer suggestions for how their sneakers could change.
- Include some of your own designs.

Today's forward-thinking designers choose recyclable or biodegradable materials.

These sneakers are made from recycled plastic bottles.

MADE WITH

6

PLASTIC BOTTLES

Made of 50% recycled PET, the ReBOTL fabric in this product contains the equivalent of 6 plastic bottles.

HANG ON TO HANGERS

Hangers are usually made of metal, plastic, wood, or a mix of these materials. Clothing stores and dry cleaners often offer customers hangers, which many people toss when they get home. But there are good reasons to hang on to your hangers.

Hangers are extremely difficult to recycle. Wooden hangers are often covered with a varnish, which is a shiny coating that makes it difficult to use the wood again. Plastic hangers are usually made from a mix of different plastics, and mixed materials like these are difficult and time-consuming to recycle. Metal hangers need to be recycled as scrap metal. As a result, clothes hangers often pile up in landfills.

Hangers are handy for hanging but horrible if they wind up in the landfill.

What a Waste!

Up to 10 billion hangers are produced around the world every year, but only about 15 percent of those hangers are recycled.

Plastic hangers are among the more than 8 million tons (7 million MT) of plastic that ends up in the world's oceans every year.

What can you do to help reduce hanger waste? You can politely refuse hangers if they are offered. Your closet is probably full of hangers already, so keep the ones you already have to hang up anything new. Use your hangers as long as possible. If you have the choice, new hangers made from recycled cardboard or recycled plastic are great lower-waste options. If you have old hangers you don't need, see if you can give them to someone who will use them.

Warriors Can Try:

See if any places in your community could use your unwanted hangers.

- Ask stores and dry cleaners if they can reuse hangers you return.
- Give hangers to local thrift stores so they can hang donated clothes.
- Ask schools and theater groups if they need hangers for their costumes.

Clothing store owners can help the environment by reusing hangers instead of giving them to customers.

Find a good new home for your hangers whenever possible.

Eco-Activity
Fashion Upcycle

If you have a stained old T-shirt, don't toss it! Turn it into a reusable bag. This way you're solving two waste problems at a time—keeping new plastic bags out of the world and upcycling old clothes!

You will need:

- An unwearable old T-shirt without large holes
- Sharp scissors

1 Check with an adult to make sure it's all right to use your T-shirt for this project.

2 Turn the T-shirt inside out and then lay it on a flat work surface. Cut the sleeves off your T-shirt, being sure to leave behind some shoulder fabric.

3 Cut around the T-shirt's neck to widen the opening a little. This will be the open end of your bag. Make sure you leave 2–3 inches (5–7.5 cm) of the T-shirt's shoulders in place—these will be your bag's handles.

4 The bottom of your T-shirt will be the bottom of the bag. Line up the front and back of the shirt. Make a fringe along the T-shirt's bottom edge by cutting through both layers of fabric upward from the bottom hem. Make the strips of the fringe about 4 in (10 cm) long. Each strip should be about 1 in (2.5 cm) wide.

5 Match the bottom and top layers of your strips. Then, double knot each back strip to each front strip.

6 Starting from the left, double knot the left most strip to the strip to its right. Then, tie the next strip to the strip to its right, working all the way across the bottom.

7 Turn the T-shirt over and repeat the process, tying each strip to the strip directly to its right.

8 Turn your bag right side out, so the knots are on the inside. You're done!

Glossary

biodegrading the breaking down of waste by living things, such as bacteria and fungi

carbon dioxide an invisible gas in the air that is released when fossil fuels are burned

climate change the change of Earth's climate and weather patterns, including the warming of Earth's air and oceans, due to human activities

coal a solid fuel found in the ground that is made from the remains of animals and plants that lived long ago

compost rotted food and other natural materials that can be used to feed soil

cotton a fabric made from the fluffy seed heads of the cotton plant

fibers threads or strips from which cloth is woven, braided, or knitted

fossil fuels fuels made from the remains of animals and plants that lived long ago

fuel a material that can be burned to make heat or power machines

global warming an increase in the temperature of Earth's air and oceans, largely caused by human activities

landfills pits where waste is dumped and then covered by soil

microfibers fibers too small to be seen by the human eye

natural fabrics cloths made from fibers found in nature, either taken from plant parts or animal hair

natural resources useful materials found in nature, such as plants, water, metals, and coal

oil also called petroleum; a liquid fuel found in the ground that is made from the remains of dead animals and plants

plastic a material, usually made from oil, that can be shaped when soft, then sets to be hard or flexible

pollution any harmful material that is put into the ground, air, or water

recycle to collect, sort, and treat waste so it is turned into materials that can be used again

upcycled having turned old materials or products into new items

Read More

Eamer, Claire. *What a Waste! Where Does Garbage Go?* Toronto: Annick Press, 2017.

Gogerly, Liz. *Go Green!* Minneapolis: Free Spirit Publishing, 2019.

Mulder, Michelle. *Trash Talk! Moving Toward a Zero-Waste World (Footprints).* Custer, WA: Orca Book Publishers, 2015.

Yates, Jane. *Cool Crafts with Cloth (Don't Throw It Away . . . Craft It!).* New York: Rosen Publishing, 2018.

Learn More Online

1. Go to **www.factsurfer.com**
2. Enter "**Clothing Warrior**" into the search box.
3. Click on the cover of this book to see a list of websites.

Index